dom' chara,

Bill Felton,

le mórmheas ⁊ baochas,

Dáithí Ó hÓgáin   2002

do Chaitríona
le grá buan

**FOOTSTEPS
FROM
ANOTHER WORLD**

Dáithí Ó hÓgáin

FOOTSTEPS
FROM
ANOTHER WORLD

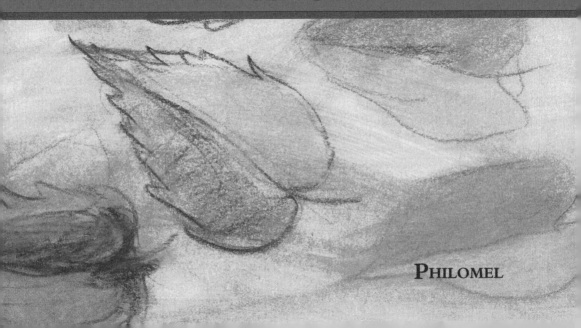

PHILOMEL

FOOTSTEPS FROM ANOTHER WORLD

by
Dáithí Ó hÓgáin

First edition 2001
Published by **Philomel Productions Ltd**

Philomel Productions Ltd
England contact address:
No 1 Queen's Gate Place Mews
London SW7 5BG, U.K.
Tel.: ++44 (0) 20 7581 2303
Fax: ++44 (0) 20 7589 2264
Ireland contact address:
E–mail: oriagain@gofree.indigo.ie

ISBN 1 898685 30 4

British Library Cataloguing in Publication Data
A catalogue record for this book is available from the British Library

TABLE OF CONTENTS

PART I - SETTING OUT

PART II - THE ENCOUNTERS

PART III - THE LESSONS

PART IV - WORDS OF EXPERIENCE

PART I - SETTING OUT

ALL THE ONE

He who goes on a long journey,
before he reaches the head of the course
will meet a stranger on the road…

The stranger moves faster,
more intensely, his knife
cuts through reefs and realms of paper
on its journey straight through life.

So one enquires of the stranger
who he is or whence he came,
and the question and answer
are always the same.

The question is the answer,
alike to the traveller…

In the answer lurks danger,
a smooth-moving stranger…

OTHER JOURNEYS

My ship slips away from the harbour
as the day begins to brighten,
glides steadily over the water,
blue, and grey as one looks
into the deeper recesses far below, far,
then heads right out to sea.

It moves in the shade of great green hilltops,
on and on,
by sun-kissed mountains
tipped by cysts of old tumuli
hiding their whispered secrets on high,
passing by misty towns on ever more distant shorelines –
the red roofs of houses, red squares on a dizzy board –
the crisscrossing roads with their mouths to the water
drinking the spirit and restless cold craving,
and away out in the wildness where nothing can save us,
running by jaws opening up in the deep
which breathe bubbled froth from a lost world
beneath,
and then thinking only of life on the surface
we silently slide with restored confidence
on through the glowing white icebergs,
and as evening falls
we find our way mid the storm-crests
as the dark sky backs up to
where we intended to sail.

But we make our way through,
and come to another harbour,

where voices with many strange accents await us,
accents measured in tone

– accents unknown
soon become our own.

POINTS IN TIME

Here is one place,
and there are many other places,
many is the hill and hollow in the poem
on the road
as it passes through many mouths
– that of the child staring
who has gone astray in the depths of winter
neath a threatening black sky in thick and heavy rain,
or the opened mouth of a desolate and dizzy old man
stumbling all over the place,
a trouble to everybody
and with all shame gone
while the sun's fearsome eye lashes the sore sand –

and, stretching out from them on every side
run the footprints.

THE CAUL-CHILD

Out of the water
the person is born,
from the quiet vastness,
from the great darkness
where lies in protection
from hate and from light
the red cap of happiness.

You were on top of the waves,
your screaming was that of triumph,
in your hand the fish of knowledge
– your own, your very own
gift from nature.

When you came into the world
the present knew you, you knew it;
though solitary you were not alone,
heroes accompanied you
– Morann, Maon, and Fionn.

A red bordering between coldness and growth
in the womb are you;
a bubble of wisdom bursting
through the freezing ice are you;
the rhythm of fire kindling
in the mind are you,
shooting sparks to the living breast
fierce and new.

THE SHORT RAMBLE

Grass grows early on each side of the footpath,
the strong yellow orb hangs like a stone,
the screen of mid-day rubbed gently by fingers
– walking towards the dawning alone.

Every blade of that grass is blazing with scorn,
the red juice oozes from the sphere split and torn,
fingernails scraping at a still screen of morn

… my back towards the slow-dying sunflower.

PICTURES AND QUESTIONS

The black raven is sharp in flight
cutting through a crimson sky,
directly deftly designedly
– what is the message in that?

And in the midst of the vast sand
on horseback there rides a man,
seeking his way through a desert of redness,
as the outlines shift
into the air, into numberless grains
– as the lines once more retract.

Will the colours reign intact,
or what is even the meaning
of that?

RUMOUR FROM THE FARM

The little boy called Cearbhall, who was herding on the mountains, got the taste of the milk of the brindled cow which gave the power of speech:–

Of all the drinks you ever quaffed
why would you not trade it for gold,
since it was not beer, nor ale,
nor power, nor learning,
nor the very water of life itself,
but only milk…
the clean and sensuous milk?

Or was it the cow which caused it,
she who strayed always to the corners,
when the rest of the herd stood unabashed before you
showing their dugs,
and because she grazed at the edge of the field
a sparkle,
inevitable
grew through her yield?

Oh, you let your mind run riot on that day
while you were on the hill,
you received an order from your master
but did not obey him,
but instead you turned the vessel upside down
and let the liquid flow right out –
every single drop riveted
deep into the mind –
so that the wheel of intellect was turned,
and your features lit up with delight,
the words came precisely to you,

figures walking strongly and directly.

And archaic things made sense to you
as well as the new
– you were the lone hero
sitting on the rudder of his boat
as white sails like the wings of great birds
ploughed the waves,
driving the gravel to the surface
and the froth to the sea-bed,
and the little fish with the whales came to look,
and all the adventures of life raced by you
like athletes skimming along the surf –
back through the flickering lights of history
as the years slipped up
to a halt
and then went in the opposite direction to usual,
wending their way
through the sturdy strongholds of chieftains
and through rooms bright and spotless,
through the strings of harps
and shadows on the ceiling,
passing by fields filled with white red-eared cows,
and the brave bull
striding out
as he heads towards the meeting of three boundaries
to face his opponent
eternal.

All your vision moved back
through every line written in loneliness,
through every adventure in legend,
through the quiet otherworld places of Ireland,
as the shining book burned out its light,
and the cure brightened and then dimmed the eyes
of the man setting out on his endless wandering through towns,
and every syllable of prophecy
spoken in secret.

Dripping like water over a mill-wheel,
or like the murmur in the mouth of a waterfall,
or like a sparkle in a dark glass of wine,
came the poetry;
through the dew of the morning seeping

came the wonders,
you imagined and pondered
the beauty of a star piercing through a fog,
the fortune came
and the misfortune
through it...

IN A REFLECTING GLASS

What is everything...
what is all that reverberates
in the shouts of children in the street
on an autumn evening
to him who stands inside a window?

Some sharp, some throated,
others shake with emotion,
opening their new paragraph,
their new clear writing on the air...

The youngest hopes embodied
as they watch their bigger peers,
the teenagers fermenting
with the ripening of years,
the bubbles of life
from the depths of all springs
find their straying way...

Looking through the solemn window
he sees all the square around,
and every body moves unceasing
as a profile on the sound,
in the shadows of the evening
chain-bound,
and the wildness is contained now
as the tolling comes all over,
a heavy bell
like a cover on the frown,
face behind a cowl

which all but the few obey…

The children always busy
must yield yet to the past,
none but the voices
ever really last…

PROMISING CLIMATE

The sheep are on the hillside grazing,
mixed in the mist, treading green gauze,
each white dot there is interest
with each new arrangement on the sward.

And as for me, I register the pole
standing so soundly
in the dumb centre of the field –
what price stability now?

FOUND AND LOST

This black-and-white stone castle
looming over the lake,
the turrets are pennoned with purple bunting
which leaps with the invisible sweeping,
the inspiration of the sighing breeze,
so that the water is diminished below
and has come to be little more than a pool.

And the narrow room is there,
the solitary library
where all your knowledge lies hidden.

The room shudders and shakes
as if struck by a far earthquake,
reverberating through the doorways,
like an uninvited guest,
like a great and sudden wind,
and the large thick-set volume moves
on the shelf on high,
slides off,
goes clear through the open casement
leaving no reflection on the glass,
trips over the proud old stone sill,
then falling
revolving
down
way down to the water,
disappearing from sight
almost before it has been seen...

Clean pages are destroyed and torn,

the etched leather cover is broken,
and the room above more lonely than ever,
its spirit locked behind a door, a cellar…

Another book
which had been left on the table
is crying out,
is burning now…

THE FAIRY HOST

The valley between the two peaks
this is called –
this is what it is called,
this valley.

Up on each peak is a village of spirits,
where the inhabitants work, trade, and play,
but never fail
to watch each other every day.

They live outside of us,
but though they can always see us,
they look down perhaps but rarely,
look down perhaps with telescopes,
on our struggles here below.

And the strange thing is
they don't seem to care so much,
although we imagine that every job we do,
every arrangement we make,
every contract
is so important
– their eyes are mostly
watching each other,
the eyes of rivals
fearing, ready to make the first move,
staring in a level line from peak to peak,
from one village to another
which never meet…

DON'T MISS YOUR CHANCE

Everything has its smell,
smells of markets long ago,
dung and shouts and chatter,
the smell of hurling,
heat and orders, pain and clatter,
the smell of the races
where all the tents are drowned
from rain and piss and drink
and mud and tickets,
the knife-like odour of equine sweat,
of competition.

Smell of a quiet chapel,
scent of lingering incense,
old and useless,
and smell of stories
pungent with age.

All speeds up now
and youth itself no longer is a memory,
no more than this gnarly young bull
which gallops by our side as we sit safely in the cart,
the rope from his head tied to the shaft,
his heavy feet pulled a little too fast
as he runs angry and helpless
and I rub his head with my hand.

'Do not be too early or too late,'
said the farmer,
'a yearling is the best time to apply the knife,

because then the strength won't be lost with the balls!'
And you can be sure that the farmer is right,
as surely as the smell of blood
is already pouring through the animal's nostrils
and mine.

This bull who has need to understand
the early and the late of it,
I fear that he is quite indifferent
to all but the scent of a heifer

indifferent to it all.

DOWN TO EARTH

Great is the excitement
for the little one,
and the boundless hope in flight
over the green grassland,
but such lasts only a moment
and the insignificant bird falls
under the hawk's onslaught,
with broken back to the sodden black earth,
a quite ordinary event.

Our days of ploughing
which must be done,
with force and roughness,
with no respite or pity,
even when the tiny torn bird
jumps in sudden starts
held by an invisible iron band
and by the desperate pulsations
in the clogged extinguishing of a heart.

A DREAM

A man dreamt
three nights running
that a treasure was hidden –
tittering gold and winking gems –
in a silver casket
somewhere deep in the earth,
and on the third night
it was revealed to him,
the exact location
– by a bridge
where four streams meet
and the moonlight beams.

Taking a spade and shovel
and a bag big enough for the task
he went there alone,
peering first through his creaking door
to make sure that nobody saw
as he departed;
he travelled through the night,
as the moon looked on
in curiosity,
and nothing interrupted him
except the owls in surprise
calling out as he passed,
a peculiarly hunched figure,
through the tall trees of graveyards
and other dark places.

He walked the long road
until he came to its end

where it branched off into a boreen
which opened into a field,
and at the end of the long field
found the first stream,
followed it to its source...

but had to return, of course.

Then he scratched his head and thought it all out
– he must go back by the same stream
and listen to its voice
as it grew louder,
follow its directions;
and, as he might have known, it brought him on
and introduced him to its friends,
the other three rivulets, all with different accents
as they came from different parts,
and met there to consult,
and the moon presiding over all
with its officious gaze,
drenched all with its condescending rays.

He first cut a circle
with the spade, stabbing the quiet clay,
and then began to dig,
only once he stopped to draw his breath,
and soon after that
he hit something,
uncovered something
– the gold screamed and the gems shivered
as his hand reached down towards them,
the first touch in so long...

Then he heard behind
the clatter,
then the raging noise,
and turned and saw the angry thing
viciously approaching,
he made to run but could not,
his feet frozen, wouldn't move for him
– the force pushed in on the circle,
mocking dark wings engulfed it,
banged it, shoved it, scraped at it,

but couldn't penetrate it.

So he had to stay all night
out in the depth of the black countryside,
and when quiet morning grew
from the orb in the east,
and a distant cock crew,
and the morning came too quietly,
he was left all dishevelled
with broken spade and shovel...

And the farmer, collecting his cows,
asking who, why, how,
and what was he up to?

ENIGMA

*A very rhetorical Irish poet once claimed that
only the crows could understand his words...*

One evening late
as the grass grew wet and jealous

the air was red
and the clouds depressed

a tree bare-branched
wounded the sky

and a black crow flew
from the horror...

HISTORY'S CROWN

They gathered around you,
all these children in a circle,
as if you were their king
– you, a mere child
among others.

And they laid on the rough ground
all their coats,
so that you could sit there,
coming all around you,
and they set with pride on your brow
the brilliant white posies,
flecked with red roses,
the crown.

They stood all around you,
inspecting you –
the white ribbons danced in the breeze
brightening up the fields,
and all the village reverberated
with the calls of willing servants
who organised your every need.

And the man who was passing by
on his own business on the road,
was kidnapped by them in sport
and brought with no delay
to show his dutiful respect
to the king of the day,
to do homage.

And my head is searing
with the white-hot blood-drops
from the pumping thorns
driven with the self-same gestures,
but with smiles much more crude
and by hands more experienced,
into the long-haired youth…

… the lingering memory
of a promise without a palace,
of a king who never ruled.

PUTTING OUT THE HAG

In the middle of Ireland it is said that the hag-spirit, a strange little animal, is driven before them by the harvesters and banished from the fields each autumn:

Drowned in a sunshower
stands the field of wheat,
stirs its golden soul,
a tremor racing through it,
fear as if alive,
the timid sprite of summer
retreating from time.

But its movement is measured
as it slips away
to its lonely place,
from the world which enters
its warren full of secrets
and strips them naked.

And another spirit is at hand,
conceived in the restless city,
growing from the rubbish yards of houses
and from smoking factories,
a spirit swelling with confidence,
multi-coloured all-embracing
garish quick-nosed ever-pacing.

Through the field of slaughter at full speed
from the bristling machine a spirit flees,
through the field of slaughter hurriedly
the second spirit comes and leers...

PART II - THE ENCOUNTERS

PASSING BY

Racing smoothly along the dual carriageway
to the womb of the city at breakneck pace,
a straight stiff line lives all the way,
and the censuring eye must surely fail.

A reddish cloud rises in copious mood,
strong magic, wide and clutching that,
weaving sturdy cosy fabric full of rules,
a hole goes deep in the heart.

O maiden moon who shines so bright,
boldly at the base of a knife-torn sky,
virgin you are to every eye

– how long will it be
till you too lose pride?

QUESTIONS AND ANSWERS

I go to the closet and take out my raincoat,
fetch my galoshes and pick up the umbrella,
although the sun is shining outside.

I walk three miles to the nearest supermarket,
and buy six packets of cigarettes,
although I have stopped smoking.

Then when I come home,
lift the latch and open the door,
I meet myself in the hallway,
with umbrella and raincoat
on my way out to the supermarket
to buy cigarettes;
and I ask myself why,
since the day is fine,
and there is a shop around the corner,
and I don't even smoke.

And I reply
– the other one, of course –
who knows?

MEETING THE OLD SEER

Between the general and the specific,
these two very sombre figures
are always speaking with a private air
outside of earshot everywhere,
but still we feel
that if we could but catch their ear
we would have nothing left to fear,
we would somehow not be taken,
no longer be conned,
a hundred and one of our problems
would be solved.

From this hill over across the great expanse,
by a clump of trees, by stream, by land,
the contoured face of Fionn Mac Cumhaill is there,
the old two-faced one,
his hunting-hounds straining at the leash
and the elusive deer
racing softly through the morning.

Between a view so free
and my step of fatigue,
through the same
unchanged
landscape
trudging,
while my face wallows in sweat
and my tattered clothes stinking wet…

DAY AT THE RACES

In a picture held at a distance
I see myself
caught by a mother's hand
striding out on a pathway
full of the world
as the traffic cuts closely by.

The direction is circular,
road and pathway winding around,
continuous unbroken both within and without,
the life-stirred approaches,
colleagues, neighbours to the town.

And outside of the house-clusters,
in the ancient countryside
a tall shopstore
stands alone in its pomp,
and within it is sombre,
each counter a circle too
as I walk around it,
and the toys are of plastic —
men, lorries, and horses.

The road a semi-circle from here,
all the way back to the roof-ends,
over the bridge and the water
and all the hidden pipes and powerlines
to the cardiac centre
where the people live;
but in this shop
the riders are on the horses,

and I there between them
walking among them, looking down,
and urging them on.

On the other side of town
the riders in splendour,
tough horses are exhausted
on their circuit eternal.

A VISION

In my room
in bed, half-sick half-well,
long is the silence
as I watch a chimney
through the window,
and a crow flying eastwards…

ONE LITTLE PERFORMANCE

When the curtain was drawn back on the lowest of all stages,
there they were in spotlight strong the children's shining faces,
the school-class brightened by the praise of all.

The little laughs of wonder,
the sweet song, out of tune,
and you there in the heart of them
like the dying note of old suspense
which had tormented you
all day through.

Every mouth spoke then, but you,
pertly loud unceasing,
and I saw your small head swinging,
and your eyes searching always
– beauty hidden is so uneasy.

And I alone had power of hearing
as the tiny cry forced its way,
timid wan-faced refugee
running right and left through the stranger crowd,
all the way to me.

Ailment of my own,
oh, once again approach!

ALWAYS YOU

Don't you think it strange how you lay dying
when all the town was full,
laden with its many voices,
and the sun was shining?

The man who agreed a way with grief,
and fought the awkward tussle
with the sour and sneering hunger,
the work that others' money screened,
and the pride that shyly suffered
the many unspoken words –
yet walked a hero through all,
never bowing or doffing,
when the race came to the call
and the sweat was choking,
the purple edges,
the sculpted ledges…

the world faded to whiteness,
all the town stood still,
and your face brightened…

CHESS IN EAMHAIN

The game of life goes on,
men move alone by turn
on the chequered board through all its colours,
and leaning over them are two figures
rubbing the sun away from their eyes,
then fingers move, twitching with tension,
measuring all the way to the edges of the board,
and the battle rages on
some distance away
unheeded.

– all the while
a woman strides her way
through a lonely race
which will finish with the day –

And so until the board is taken up again,
brought out to a bright lawn with the dawning,
and a different couple sit down
to the table with its chequered board
and all its colours…

FEAR IN THE TOWN

I fear the streets at night,
that they might explode, might scream,
might speak a language I can't understand,
that they might begin to move before me,
might rock, might rattle,
might go quietly away,
and that I might hear a footbeat
from a different world...

PRESENT FROM ANOTHER REALM

The cold ice on every side,
tall trees are shaking in the sturdy breeze,
the gleam of snow from the vision's source,
and I remember no more of the portrait,
except a gold ring which was left on the stone
sparkling there alternately big and small,
less and more…

That made a spectrum
which engirdled the plain,
two colours here mingling
surpassing all paint;
and the tracks of the travelling,
and the hooves of my horse,
through the end of hard winter,
deep black in the frost,
dim my sight as I pass…

PEGASUS

A slim steed is in the mind,
his teeth a whetstone.

His ears a handle, laid back,
his neck is an arch,
work of the hands of masterbuilder,
a high-powered cadillac
ready to gallop away,
but will it?

His nostrils distended
burning with coldness,
his breath full of pain
groans on the air,
combing his mane
and his step
straightening in high dudgeon.

From legs up to shoulder
muscles knotted and taut,
savage yet electric
the veins are all caught.

Vein of speed in his movement,
vein of madness in his head,
vein of bareness in his bold pride,
vein of flaming in his sperm.

Wild steed of my mind,
fierce stallion in thought...

MY TWO DWELLINGS

... in my father's house there are many mansions ...

I really don't know at all what caused me
to hire this builder
to erect a new house at the bottom of the garden –
a house just like the other one –
unless it was the troubled ghost
who made its nest up there inside,
coming in a puff of wind through the stairway,
playing my piano in the dead of night,
and ceaselessly looking at farces on the telly,
not to mention gobbling all my food in the pantry.

But it was when he had the audacity
to trip me up one morning in the hallway
and I late for work already
that I finally decided irrevocably
to build the other house.

And what good is that for me now?
What good really in the long term?
When my descendants will once again settle
in the first house – the natural place of course –
which has the same type of site and construction
as all the other houses in the estate
as they now and again look out
on the gaping road of fate.

But this new one
at the bottom of the garden
in the deserted spot,

not to mention the steep drop
to the country road behind it...

There are no steps going there either,
so that there is hardly a choice
but to plunge down headfirst
to the dirt-track twenty feet below
on the other side of the mudbank –
how awkward for shopping purposes
with all the neighbours watching?

Yet who can tell?
Perhaps it would be a shortcut,
help me avoid the long way around –
even though the traffic would be skidding along the verge,
and the County Council has no plan as yet
to put a footpath there...

All of which means
that I still must
come around the gable of the first house –
by the gable of the proper natural house –
just as I am already doing once a week
with the rubbish-bin...
once a week?
And the gate must be left open...
the gate must be left open?

Just so, it is the selfsame trip
from the old house to the new one,
and the two dwellings look exactly the same...
but do I want them to be exactly the same
if I have to have a private footpath
all the way through the garden?

My very own footpath between the two dwellings,
I will be walking along there
on my little private property in seclusion from the world...

And when above in the old house
the ghost sees that,
and how convenient it is,
I fear that he will follow my example,
that he will give his chain a shake,

that a glimmer will come in his eye,
that he will rattle his teeth
and let out a bellow,
and move down here himself...

TO AND FRO, UP AND DOWN

Sink down the pendulum
towards the dense solution,
into the hidden pores,
moving backwards and then forwards
in the gathering time
in the growing dusk,
still always like
a child left out alone
in his cold night.

This elevator with a bar misplaced
which keeps it from rising too high,
or from going quite
into the depths
where dwells the wound amid scorching flame,
where winks the brain in its pulpy grave.

Not reaching quite into the surging mass
where ruin follows ruin and sense rules not
but from which come more forms anew,
some smart, some mangled –
the hidden place
for which never tiring
madness raps upon the door
seeking fame and more and more,
seeking entry loud with shouts,
but the lift goes down quite sudden,
quite unexpectedly,
and in its drop
clears all before it,
dispersing

dissipating
the sulphur clouds.

And time itself goes on before,
kind stranger who remains remote
but nods
and moves his lips –
new taste is ripe and sight not sore,
all the secrets yet unknown…

The cold ice spreads around the fire,
together raise the silent cry…

STATUES IN A ROW

A joyful statue on the edge of the city
a watch on everything that will take place
– the heavy bargains, the merry dancers, the seduction,
and the beggar's back as he walks away.

A solemn statue on the edge of the city,
at the other end also watching,
and every temptation which crosses that way
it jots down in its notebook to accusc.

That place which is the people's lives,
between the two statues so quiet.

OLD AND NEW

Up there by the water-works
where the road narrows into the big forest
– the man said to me quietly
as if in confidence –
you will find the herd of bison,
a fog of breath ringing them
and mixing away into the dusk of the trees.

Up there at the reservoir
and dam
where black water rages,
trundling, then racing down from the massive valves
– feat of intellect from the hand of man
nurturing, cultivating, assuring...

While the ancient bison
grazes quietly in the mist...

THE GIFT

'Give the dolly to me,
let it go –
you have the other thing,
the rattler,
for yourself!'

'Don't, it's mine,
you got enough already
out of the silver box
that she left behind in her room –
and even the room itself and the coloured pillow
and the beautiful schoolbag,
you got them all!'

'Listen, I've said it before,
and must I repeat myself...?'

'And Mammy agreed...
she remembers...
the doll is mine!'

'It's yours, what am I hearing!
And you seven years of age now...
she was only five,
and if I don't get what is mine by right,
since it wasn't buried along with her,
and since she promised,
and since...
that doll should be... should be...
should in fairness be...
burned!'

'Poor Noreen, and she gone from us,
and ye trying to wreck the arrangement
and to take it away from me –
it was to me that she left it,
don't ye remember her that evening in the bed –
she is looking down at ye all now –
remember, isn't that what she said,
what Noreen herself said,
the instructions she left!'

'You little grabber, let go your grip,
give it to me,
give it to me…
I wiped the drops from her forehead,
and she said that that doll would be mine!'

'Boo-hoo, she gave it to me from her own two hands,
I fell in for it!'

'She said…'

'Look, I tell you, it's mine…'

'Give it to me at once…'

'I'll tear…'

'Noreen said it was mine!'

NOISE AND GLORY

Prancing and dancing
in the mouth of the great ball we go,
the golden mass of dawning,
the bright ring of day,
delighted,
making merry
through living snow on every side,
conversing with each other in excited roars
and playful shouts
and peals of laughter.

And you, little shaggy horse,
I speak to you also,
you who were left out in the bitter winter
as the frost took bites out of you,
out of your sides and your belly,
holed you through the skin
and through the sinews and bones
all the way into the heart,
as the years grew up on you
your legs and muscles stiffened
and your teeth were worn black down to the gums.

All of this winter-play we have,
this jolly laughter and joy in the mountain camp,
the sport and all the postures,
the hectic circle
– I would change it all if I could
so as to bring the spring back to us,
for your sake, little gelding of the dead dark eyes,
who was left out in the cold too long…

And not because you brought the hero to the Land of Youth,
Oisín who smiled and laughed with Niamh;
and not because you carried Roland on your back
in the valley of death at Roncesvalles;
and not because you brought the Hound of Tricks to safety
from the long drawn-out moan of slaughter
when you sharpened your teeth on the flesh of the enemy;
and not because you might perhaps have once been Arkle
or the spotted Tetrarch wonder
who always changed his colour
and rocked with vigour when he hit the front,
or Secretariat huge stallion
who turned out barren
only for a while
– none of these you were
who swept away ahead of all your species
with ears laid back
filled with the cheers of the crowd,
racing forever into the treasure chest of memories,
no, not at all!

But because you are yourself,
shaggy little horse,
going to his death in the cold of winter.

BY A CASTELLATED WALL

Over there lies the sloping,
sharp and sudden fencing all around the spoils,
steam rising hot from the flanks of the thickened herd,
and boldly in their midst
the commander bull
looking up and around –
his red eye reads the circle,
then turns,
and from between his hind legs
the fore hoof on the right can be seen
scraping the clay into a wave of blood.

He amidst the cows
stolen from the chieftain to the south,
and the bullocks on the offside
furthest from the fort
are standing just under the stakes –
their profile is still and sullen
as the swarthy clouds overhead,
the guards too are sulking,
their faces scarcely move
and their spears have cut into the horizon.

Long ago a pulse was beating –
long ago as we say now –
steam and mist and seed and stamping,
sweat and tears and wealth and weeping,
a thousand years through pages bleeding
colours our picture in for us,
as the terrain itself is restless,
stirs and strives

to waken,
makes its one great move
to return…

THE TWIN BROTHERS

The feast was in full swing,
  the cups were being drained,
when he struck against the door
with a heavy thud,
a force from somewhere in the night outside,
oh, so unmannerly,
and pushed his way into the company
of skilled and practiced heroes,
and he so gnarled and dour of mien.

In his horrible rags
he trampled to the table,
where his clean brother sat
firmly in control of all.

Only the dog came to meet him,
and then all sat still
in no small degree of indignation
as he was upbraided
and questioned minutely and properly −
what happened to his men,
that troop given to him
to prevent the raiders.

'I left them where I left them
on the head of the strand and in the valleys deep,
in the great forest which shakes with age,
and in the cold morning early
lying in perpetual sleep −
that is what happened to my band,
defending their purpose,

while you sit fat
and sated
and drink deep!'

All sat silent, looking each to one side,
while the two pairs of eyes met,
not knowing
whether to kiss or to fight...

THE MAD MONK

You were the martyr,
and when I looked out
through the doorway that morning
as I spoke of you
the sun was brilliant,
splitting to the very hearts of stones,
and my theme for the students
was in pieces too.

And for a while I thought
of an unclouded sky
so brilliant,
and of your torment being equal
to one who enjoys
all the pleasures of the world
while still full of longing, slowly,
through a glass of dead delight
in the cloister
where the saints abide.

Joy and some pleasure
in every face there
of all the listeners,
and yet as I speak
through the hammering and drilling outside,
in the long tormenting noise
of barking drills
which distresses all but me so little
another phantom will arise.

You a lonely man forgotten,

you who once fed wolves,
and led the lark in song as it climbed
higher and higher,
you who did the heavy penance
there in the water
at every circling of the mountains,
at every turning of the sky,
standing to your very neck
in the water
unbroken,
looking at death inch closer
for weeks on end,
through every night
and day passing
in the lake cold,
spiritless,
and wide.

THE REQUEST

They told me when they returned
from the long search with their knives
that they had neither seen nor met anything
in their thirsty travels
but the agile stranger
who had walked straight up to them
and asked no boon
when he was overcome
but a trim and neat coffin
with just enough room inside,
and by a white horse drawn…

WATCHING THE DEAL

The cards go all around flicking
in the circuit like the hands of a watch,
the same distance between each flat,
as the breaths of the players go silent –

all the backs the same before the eyes
which wait for the trump to rise...

A VISION LATE

A vision late I saw
last night in a house
of dusk.

A man in years
and a bent old woman
in an empty kitchen
where a broken table stood,
one leg standing out from the board,
a jagged outpost at the end of war.

And on the wall some writing
about some day of birth or other –
the elderly man taking
a box from his pocket,
brittle with rust
and leaving it on the broken table.

A hundred other years, maybe,
or close upon it,
of giving and taking
made the box mouldy
and empty, quite empty.

As if it were some game,
repeated solemnly each date.

A NOTE IN THE AIR

Walking out of the church
on a bright summer evening,
as the weakened sun slipped down through shadows
on the narrow streets between the red houses
on every side,
and the sound of prayers in syllables
linking the crown of the Virgin on the world.

The blue sky standing over all,
the circle of bright clouds in its centre
white as snow
walking slow
and slowly moving around,
so that the prayers themselves seemed to be turning
– taking us back
from the streets and houses
away by the hour
into the years,
and into the generations,
and back yet further
from the ages to the epochs
through withering and growing
of quiet forests.

The movement never ceased
until we returned again to blue heaven and white clouds,
and all was still,
as I gazed at the trees,
at the heart of a wood
on the edge of a new-hewn mountain,
and a circle of bleached skulls laid on the ground,

skulls of huge creatures,
a dumb ritual
by silent men
for quiet Mary,
for our ancient lady,
for her gentle smile
and white blue-shaded eyes

our lady of the mammoths…

EXPLORATIONS

From where I presently stand
I long to…
out of sheer curiosity, you see,
long to start just here and
take a walk
down along the twisting avenue
with the bushes to one side all in flower,
all bare and naked on the other,
walking on determinedly
until I pass the signpost at the bottom
and go around the final corner.

I will enter through the rattly rusty gate
and go inside
this garden of mine
to discover
all within,
and there is only one condition –
I must skirt around by the back of the building,
and make no sound.

While trotting thus through the archway
I cannot help but notice the dark corners here and there
moistened by the drip of time,
brightened by the odd shaft of light;
I will stop for a few seconds
there on the last line of sanity
and look out from within and smile
and welcome weary passers-by
who through no fault of their own
have come here likewise

– except of course for the odd one I cannot like –
and curtsy briefly and with my hand direct
all whom I can tolerate in this clime.

In this land,
the well-ploughed worn-out furrow
of a million useless thoughts,
of ten times more desires
which still incline to come alive
and walk through day and night,
moving about from wall to wall obliquely,
in the damp silence, in the lush greenness,
in the clear violets, in the bleakness –
some speak curtly to each other,
others in gentle soothing tones,
others are still yet
not even on speaking terms,
but all are within, where a slow sun shines –
a sun all to itself –
red and pulsing,
so red and so pulsing as to nauseate –
which dies, and then is born again.

And I never wish out of curiosity
to take a second walk in the world outside,
but fall asleep and waken again to it,
and see all the twisting tubes and wires,
and pipes and bellows,
and all the engines moving, and all the lights.

PART III - THE LESSONS

NOISES AT NIGHT

Dogs are barking on the other side of town,
deep and hollow one of them is entangled in the air,
the other in the thin voice born out of shivers,
and the third one with quick echoes of decision –
the skin is peeled sore from all memories of this place
by every bark and yelp and bay.

I hear the hounds sounding,
giving tongue to their world,
for all who are roughly awakened
to the difference in words;
and every corner of the town towards darkness
stirs through their throbbing throats,
and the belly of every road
grows towards me with the taste-buds of the glutton
longing to hasten away
over the highest roofs of houses,
sleek from wind and greasy rain,
over wires and over steeples,
over taverns' quiet despair.

I alone
and my hounds
on the other side of night.

SOME RUBRICS

What is that film which slips backwards by us,
 it had a dark hue,
but appearances are deceptive
– but what is this human voice we hear
which speaks and speaks but is never clear?

The word is broken early in the throat,
or, if it survives, quickly turns to scraping in the jaw –
the frozen view of a crowd of people
pushing, now a melée over there.

So we stretch out our attention
away across with such a strain
that our nerve-ends tingle,
and nothing is heard for all our hearing
but echo and more echoes again.

Behind in a protected place,
seated and sequestered, I fancy,
are those we never mention, seldom imagine,
as they sneer and scoff and slander.

WHEN THE RUSHES ARE BLACK

*A jester who had received a gift from Guaire, king of Connacht, claimed
that the king would be rewarded after the birth of Christ … well was this
fulfilled for Guaire, that on account of his generosity he was granted berries
in winter…*

The gusts of rugged weather came as usual,
blowing furiously one after the other
– unwelcome guests trying to grab the premier place –
black rain, hardy north wind,
strange grunting and groaning, and the frost!

In an instant all was stopped,
and they stood there glaring in surprise,
as the true guest came
– the day as gentle and quietspoken
as any who ever entered the hall.

And so the soft breeze blew from the south,
and the withered stalk of winter listened to his voice
and longed for the past,
sliding back in memory
through its multi-coloured autumn
when decay had first set in,
the gentle words were falling and then returning
speaking to the eye.

Standing stark and lively on the branch
were figures
in blue, fresh green, violet,
and above all else yellow,
and red as leaf-blood moved through veins,

all the foliage,
there in profile
as the world around sank back to oblivion.

From the prick on the stem
on this branch in front of me
the purple leaf is going to shed,
and the other bushes
have a grey colour climbing on their backs,
and I understand
that in a different way,
and if all things were in another shape,
the mulberry could begin to grow
nurtured in the womb and lap of experienced winter,
and that it would burst forth in flame
against a clean white sheet.

A promise whose fulfilment is guaranteed
by trees while they still drop leaves.

BOOKS FOR SALE

That pedlar at the market in town
sells books by the dozen
in bags and boxes and torn packets
bulking under his time-hacked woodwormed bench
surrounded by rags and rust and stench.

Dante can be had there, sad and merry,
with brooding portraits of the devil,
history of the slave-trade is there too,
beside Pinocchio's adventures,
and seven steps to heaven,
and the French Revolution itself remembered.

But, why, why did you take this book
from such a dirty seller,
it's full of dirt and dust
and maybe something worse…
how can it help in my exams,
what can it tell me?

It mightn't be right for the honours class,
the information could be out of date,
and anyway it probably is the wrong edition,
and even if it isn't
I don't want to be seditious,
and… and spreading germs.

And how could a book
sold at such a filthy market
have all the answers?

THE DECORATED MENU

All food which had been placed on the table
in plates and on the silver dishes
was fare which seemed so tasty
that little would be wasted,
as one guest remarked wittily
turning to his neighbour
as the company took their seats.

Then we noticed a funny twist
to the proceedings
– a woman came
and then another and another,
and sat to table one by one,
one after the other,
and ate from the same plate
quite ravenously
the half-finished fare
left by each predecessor.

And this was so,
this was the custom,
with everyone present,
all the company around.

The leavings had the toothmarks,
shell-torn gashes in clay,
and then new food was piled on top,
and all was mixed
through the offal beneath
– but those who ate
wore such pleased countenances,

so clean and peaceful
at what was laid before us,
before my own eyes and my mouth,
that I knew I had to agree
to eat or to leave…

HARSH WORDS SPOKEN

More dangerous is my whisper than the roar of a hundred men…

The man told me
that the night before
there at the turn in the mountain,
through the gap where two roads meet,
he met the rats,
a whole drove of them,
a dark cloud travelling,
squealing and pattering,
so that he had to leave the roadway
and walk along in the drain to one side.

When I asked him how this was so,
what had sent the rats about that business,
he reminded me of my poem
made the day before
which in measured verses told
of how I had been treated there;
and, of course, as I should know,
it was quite frank and fair
and rats obeyed such tones.

So this was what had sent them
in their pre-ordained direction,
acting out my strongest words,
fierce energy of my mouth,
sharper, though whispered, than any cry or shout.

Oh, yes, there was one other thing –
up ahead was an old grey one,

half-blind,
a rat hardly able to walk with age
being helped along by two strapping young fellows
whose eyes beamed with the fire of rhetoric
and the passion of the unknown,
and who had put a straw across between their mouths
on which he leant to help him on.

And so this ancient fellow was coming at the head of all,
their wise director and advisor,
their leader long established

and he was laughing…

THE SCHOOL OF MAGIC

Out after the sun
as the flames lit through our path,
the red ball twitching on the horizon,
that morning that our lives began.

The rays pouring in on us
through our eyes and sockets to the skull,
my own heart nibbled
by a creaking sound
which touched and then was gone,
calm after an unheard storm,
and the ghosts of future encounters rising up
as we walked right on and on.

Leaving the darkest school behind us
where all our magic had been learned,
and the master seeking one of us,
just one of us three
to stay another term.

But the foremost of us spoke clearly:
'Take the one behind me
who thinks this a joke,
or the next one after that
who doesn't know what it is,
but who thinks to shrink from fear to favour,
or, better still, take a look back
at that quiet one skulking
and stretching out at the rear of all!'

And so he did, that master,

took the only payment offered –
from man to man he made no profit
from all his teaching through the seasons,
found but an image in the light of day.

He, who knew the far horizons,
found no living one to stay
on which to test his art and learning,
and the three of us got clean away –
and my own shadow
rarely seen but still existing,
the last of the line,
the very gentlest yet most persistent
was already blackened
in that torrid clime.

THAT WAS WHEN

That was when I wrote the poem
that defeated all the poems
that I had ever pondered,
or anyone else to my knowledge.

But I lost it,
the horse that I could no longer ride
that raced away when I pricked its side
along the slope and down into the valley
until it came to the ledge
from which it gazed right down
into the chasm...

ON CHRISTMAS NIGHT

I hear the music coming from above,
upstairs in their version of eternity,
the angels' song,
a child's voice which knows no borders
slipping through doors,
escaping through porches
out onto the restless world
and back again to soft white sheets.

And the cry of lamentation rises
to those who listen
through the passing of these years.

IN A CHILD'S PLAYROOM

This great range is a street laid out before us,
stretching through the ancient books,
through the pages dark and brightened
down along the way of cries
– each roof a different dimension
shoving the others aside
and nodding at them briskly
to be sure and keep their distance.

A tiny bottle is on the table
standing in humble majesty
among the books and torn papers,
child of a child, the doll's sole toy,
between the painted men and women,
snakes and ladders, draughts, and quoits.

The bottle stands as one great landmark,
in the city full of meanings,
its cause, its shape, its sullied cleanness,
white liquid simulating milk half way up,
and a pink tower-cap on top.

Tower of yet another building,
tower of the world beginning.

FLECKING THE WAVES

The wind blows in a whirl around us
coming in on every side,
but it was the sudden blast which rocked us
and gave us to the tide.

The fine blue arc is soft and gentle
once the savage waves subside...

I did my time in the huge whale's belly,
and painted the white shore when I came to land
on my own wide canvas,
scanned the horizon to see just one house,
and longed for one living to take my hand,
and thereafter I decided to live like a wild one,
away from society in hollows and forests,
and hung my jacket on a smiling sunbeam
and it stood for me.

I laughed with the streams and danced with the rushes,
and even went on the tops of trees,
racing like the world's best runner
never missing a step,
never pausing for breath,
and late one evening I talked to the bees
to know what none knew but all have pondered,
I was willing to suffer and utter no plea,
yet the gods rejected me,
and left me, oh so desolate,
here.

The fine blue arc is soft and gentle

once the savage waves subside…

Now I hear the wind-man speaking,
an elderly voice
impatient,
sullen, weak yet earnest,
creaking:

'There is a smudge on my miracle
from the common hoof broken,
now the thief's in my house
and the door is wide open!'

TWO MUTE FIGURES

There they stand so clear and knowable,
in all their nakedness,
on the hard cold flags on the floor,
the pair of sandals alone.

Their straps are well worn
from the strain of sod and cement,
on innumerable fields and roads,
and the sheen of long distanced feet on them,
and the black coat of sweat on their lips.

Telling once again
of all the effort spent.

One of them has turned to the south,
and its partner has turned west
to tell anyone who is interested
which direction
is preferred
by them.

A PAIR OF GHOSTS

A spirit has passed down by me
in the darkness of this room,
walking slowly without noticing
me at all;
and another spirit has passed up by me
sounding like a breezy tremor,
bowing to me courteously as it went by –
the two met together in the middle of the room
just as the moonlight appeared through the window.

They turned to each other,
speaking some words undecipherable,
and then both turned and looked back at me
– one lifted his finger
in reproach, or perhaps jestfully;
and the other bowed his head
with solemnity, yet hurriedly.

But those words which they spoke
can never be told…

THINGS WHICH DO NOT SPARKLE

D'aithle na bhfileadh darbh ionmhas éigse is iúl,
is mairg a chonairc an chinneamhain d'éirigh dúinn…
Dáibhí Ó Bruadair, 1682

These jewels which we fashion with our hands,
if jewels they be…
but if we didn't believe in them,
little would be our torment or our grief.

Shining they be neath greedy eyes,
or beneath the eyes of those who direct us
– one must be hard like the very gem
which once was found in the dragon's nest,
where it was cast aside on the heap
of sour-smelling straw, the corpses' keep.

Yet despite what all the learned say
they are sweet to us who bore them faint
from the gentle parts of our darkness,
from flesh and vein in dankness.

And they must still be cut to size,
while the human race its fate denies,
while lacking strength
but longing…

BIFOCAL LENSES

Eyes, someone said,
are but two orbs in the forehead,
two planets revolving
only part of the way,
and these two eyes cast light into the brain...

But they only look outwards,
and see nothing at all within...

GLIMPSES

The little chequered squares
within the big square of the window,
and I inside
in the dusk of evening
a dim shadow on the opposite wall
increasing.

On the dark grass
on the opposite side of glass,
the outside,
the little white mass is moving,
he who has one black end, the two-coloured rabbit
jerks from square to square.

Which next square will his nose attain,
when will he stop?

AT LOUGH GUR ON AN AUTUMN EVENING

Those reeds over there are like dashes in writing,
marking out the ends of the lake's strong lines,
deep in water's mirror lie their hidden verbal roots...
while their heads shake in fake shyness
and arch coyly in the wind.

When one dashing spirit
like a nervous stranger rushes through them,
they jump and stand with open mouth
in pretended shock at this irrepressible stirring
as life comes to them in sudden shapes and grooves
which cause a skirted leg to twitch and a slanting eye to move.

I see the white steed racing through the reeds,
with the cold of the evening its nostrils are filled,
the knight versed in secrets
and all the paths unseen
is spurring it on
in one crazed gallop...

A FEROCIOUS PET

That great tiger which I had,
I remember it well about the house,
sniffing and snorting, growling and hiding
just like a pet cat, but louder
– you must know that we had a massive armchair in those days.

He even used to come to drink his milk from a saucer –
a great saucer, of course, incised with bright red gold –
and he would lie down on our threshold
as night crept up,
watching the yellow moon
in the blackness without end away above,
which I fancied used to lick up his colours,
and with the approach of morning
he would come again to the hallway
and wait there for me.

Until one night
by a foolish oversight
I left the gate unlocked at the bottom of the garden,
and while we slept and conscience left
he slipped away into the unkown
– for me the moon was dreaming on high
of the warm white sheets below.

So,
when I awoke in the morning,
he was gone.

I sat to breakfast early on that day
but ate nothing, thinking all the while

that he would soon return,
I pushed the bread aside,
then I plugged the kettle in and let it burn out,
and waited again.

But he did come back
in a loping half-trot,
his belly dangling from side to side as he came
through the wide open gullet of the gate,
and licked his lips and pawed his ears
and lay again on the threshold as before;
when I ruffled his giant head
I felt the spirit of the wild country tingling,
the cold air of night which lingered
in the matted fur,
reminding me
of the cool light shaft
deep in whiskey in a glass
after a heavy night,
or the glint in a child's eye,
or a titter on the lips of an old man.

But the hue and cry soon went up
all around the town,
and by mid-day
began the chase
for a savage beast without mind or manners
which had torn the throat out of a dozen sheep
high in the hills where they had grazed at peace,
way up there in the still white snow
during the long and empty night,
the thick red blood had spurted out
with gore and black lumps through it
falling to the ground,
and the dying cries were snuffed out
by the growling all around
of the brute which could do it,
which could do such a thing...

Of course, they came straight to my house,
and without even addressing me
they seized my tiger and dragged him through the gate;
he allowed himself to be taken
but the glimmer in his great dull eyes

was fiercely asking why...

His head was jerked away
by the choking rope,
and he was lifted by six men and thrown
headlong into their lorry,
where the thick black bars
hid his yellow streaks,
and made him into one slinking dark force
except for the corners of his eyes
which shone red like gold.

I suppose they hanged him...

And a week after his death
the work on the hills began again,
a dozen more sheep
were found torn asunder,
mangled and with pink guts dangling,
swollen, stupidly soft –
the madness dripped saliva,
and its whiteness gleamed like a shade
as it fell curdling down
into some quiet mountain lake.

COLD AND THIRSTY

When the man of knowledge
in the northern zone,
going astray on the tundra,
following his calling –
from the silent unknown –
rubs his cheek and pulls at his beard,
stops for a moment and looks all around,
he sees his roof in the blue orb above him
with the sun a sharp nail driven through,
and perhaps he will notice
spreading increasing
the fingers of shadow
on full whiteness creeping.

With no food or sleep,
in a lonely cold kingdom,
tormented and tortured,
in a mad thirst for wisdom.

And when I go to solitude
it is among all the people,
through the rushing and pushing
in a city just here now –
a bicycle my reindeer,
the houses are my sky,
my ritual each morning
is a six o'clock rise,
the long drone my silence,
a streetlamp my light.

Food and sleep are all there for me,

and a shelter sure from sleet and frost,
hands encompassing yet unloving
arrange my day from dawn to dusk,
while through my thoughts are always spreading
these shadow fingers from the north,
and the voice of silence quietly reaches
through scattered icebergs in the heart.

WAITING FOR SOMETHING TO HAPPEN

The night has broken through me like projectiles,
to the core of a will which desires no writing,
glancing off a hand which shakes
decrepit
– the cruel face of failure stares up at me,
and the spoiling destroying world suffices,
is too dense,
makes no sense.

As time goes by will growth come again?
Will rubbish be collected in a shining bin?
Will broken shreds make new clear forms?
Will tasty hunger return to charm?
Will mouth speak, mind see, hand feel?
Will rot screech out from the tomb in the heart,
with the scraping stinging voice
of a demon being driven away,
with the return of day?

GOING BY HERE

Last spring these distant houses were built,
and soon the débris and all the sand were cleared away,
before long the grass began to grow again
on the edge of every road as the plans on paper said it would.

And the new inhabitants
brought new life to the place.

I remember also how my eye fell
as I drove swiftly by
on the new liss which had grown in the park
between the road and the pathways,
and how I noticed
that its colour became darker green by the day
so that by summer it was almost the same
as a rath or tumulus in the ancient countryside
which yet remained
untouched by modern man
with his harsh hands,
untamed.

Nearby the children's carousel was turning around,
until one autumn evening came,
the sort of evening when a ray of sun and a long shadow
stand alive beside each other
like neighbours who will not talk,
as I drove by I thought
that, strangely, I was further from the place,
the reason soon was clear –
the new estate
between it and the dual carriageway

– all the merry red roofs were in my mirror,
and I thought of
sparkling towers on castles of old…

And away behind,
up towards the top of my windscreen
the new liss had come into flower,
yellow and red in full bloom,
and the cemetery slabs were growing too
around its edge
white and new…

PART IV - WORDS OF EXPERIENCE

FAIRY FEET IN THE NIGHT

Along the road to the west,
where the sun goes down
behind the climbing trees
I hear the spirits coming,
and then passing by so free.

Yet, for all their bustle,
from where they come
I know not.

As a result of all this coming
what seed will blossom the land,
or what hell will lie in waiting
which a fool will find so grand?

Or what will there be for us to divide
in the place our faces find?

THE BAD BUILDINGS

O high lights
  squared in windows,
way above the town,
you are so solemn,
with no voice from the backstreets reaching you,
no titter from lovers in dark walls,
no music which winds around the corners,
no boasting, no joking,
none at all
– come down!

Come down
before it is too late,
before the end,
a futile end,
a lonely scream at night.

Come down,
even if you think it hardly worthwhile,
for the pain of bloodstreams
is clotted in us,
frozen in us,
and you would laugh if you saw
how our hands and shoulders shake,
though not with age,
and how our mouths are sealed
though not from greed.

That snigger in the ear
is not the laugh that we long for,
but the raving, roaring, ranting, revelling,

and the bare feeling
for all the people,
for holes driven through their minds,
for their souls dented
like wind–filled paper-bags,
for their blood soiled,
for their ancient thirst…

Again and again
you have scoffed,
you will be damned, high windows,
solemn over the town,
may you collapse and fall,
may your ruin amuse us all…

The poison of my mouth be on you,
bitter black drop unrefined,
the poisoned dagger of my mind!

THE GAMBLE OF TIME

Hope without failing and the gambler is ruined...

The down of winter is growing again on the cow,
her hand-delivered free-of-charge coat,
and on every other mammal
which lives up the road,
and thus it has always provided protection
through the rough road of the ages,
through every gene –
the great ox of Europe, the aurochs, the zuber,
is standing there in front of us
lowering its head and glaring,
although it last disappeared from our sight
three hundred years ago
in an eastern forest,
and the little savage dark bull
rushing from the southern range to challenge him,
and to win,
and so to leave his squat figure
in three hundred shapes around us.

The people always say
that the first two-horned came to us from the sun,
but the hand of science waves this aside
and states in deep authoritative voice
that there was a beast and a beast
and a beast on grassy soil
for the last three hundred thousand years,
accompanied by many other breeds of mammal
and innumerable breeds whose seed has dampened
and gone to dust or dirt or sandstone,

116

but all had their coats.

And the coat just came and went
measured and tailored to season
as each year turned by,
and prior to that the down came intermittently,
not quite right,
but the climate cleared that up
and the falling aside of the weak
who lacked the savage streak,
so that a million
went out of practice
and out of business,
and before that again the ox went out on its own,
and before that again the hoof was splitting,
and before that again there was no hoof but a finger,
and before that again the first pricklings
of downy hairs began to come,
a slight itching on the skin.

Before that, as the world would have it,
the mammals dissented,
and before that something moved free of soil
no longer lack-lustre and tied,
and before that began life,
quivering,
trembling with fright,
with wonder came the feeling
of wanting and of being,
and the rupture of waves with soil,
and before that, who knows why…

The coat of down keeps its shape
on the ancient hide of the cow,
who is milk and meat to all who break
with patterns of tell-you-how,
and she is leather for shoes
to walk where we choose,
and seek and search and pry
through a million
accidental designs.

THE WORLD RUSHES ON

Still we are thinking
of the great quiet forest

I cannot remember a day ever as beautiful as this –
all the elements dance and sparkle –
and I can depend on my eyes
which can without effort in this clime
see crystal clear
as along the shaft of a telescope
each blade of grass, each mountain slope
reaching away from me,
their outlines and profiles are so magnified –
stimulation!

Everything lives in the mind just now,
every business to be done is neatly filed in rows,
marked even with precise numbers,
making everything so controllable.

The fine big ball is moving on
with speed so great as not to be noticed,
and every neatly arranged planet and star far away,
never denying the music of the spheres
in their steady rush from the ancient day
when all exploded.

Every single thing walks quietly here,
but there are a million billion of worlds outside
fleeing, escaping, bellowing, shaking –
something will crash!

The eternal circle
races on its axis
at a pace of a thousand miles at least
the wheel revolves every hour...

The dregs of poison drip from a broken glass,
the bowels of the sea are rent and torn
and crimson cutting go the wind–mill arms
without let up into the dumb body of the earth,
teeth grow sharper, animals are shredded,
comrades stumble deserted in the eyes of the storm,
withered trees make tables and beds and baskets

... and never a question ever answered.

We are being flung headlong through space
at seventy thousand miles
every hour, or more
for all I know.

Something will collide
with something else
sometime,
with a mighty crash,
will detonate and bang
and burst asunder –

Some...thing...yet...will...crash...

SYLLABLES FROM THE DEPTHS OF THE BODY

Although we are dying
day by day,
how you do not know,
why I cannot say...

The green verdure on the mountain rolls,
the sentry stones on the cliffs shine,
the water laps sadly in the rivers,
the twinkling star in the evening
calls me home,
while the strong white stallions gallop on forever
hammering their hoofbeats on the plains
through the clefts and mounds and soft spots,
through the blood-red arteries of our veins...

And I will keep my secret
deep under the sod inside,
for you know I cannot speak it,
you must confide...

I cannot say,
although I am dying
every day...

RUSHING BY

From the start of silence
I hear the start of noise,
the rumbling of rubber reaches almost to the nostrils,
the car approaching on the road somewhere.

How angry it seems to be,
how destructive, perhaps how desperate,
how controlled and still how frightened,
how strong and constant, yet how pained
in its own way –
unpredictable like thunder on a gentle day
blundering through a higher roadway,
screaming as it slides awry through wetness,
generates through tarry sky,
shouldering contemptuously at pavement,
yet enclosed and sad and dry.

Suddenly the crescendo sinks and lowers,
and the dying noise stops altogether flowing,
and I know that between its coming and its going
there too has passed another stage of life.

ALL THE PEOPLE

All the people laughing,
scoffs high, scoffs low,
quaintly and heartily,
quick, measured, and slow.

Fat, thin, chesty, rambling,
uneasy peals and moans,
kind and gentle, rough and raucous,
snubby, pointy, slobbery, long-nosed

– while the worm pushes its passage underground –

the laughs die away,
and stillness reigns,
the person pays.

TO A SOCIABLE HERMIT

You look down upon the siege,
   proud and surly
from your leaning tower
in need.

And you think that the vehement army
can be pushed backwards, away from you,
by your smiles and your fondling,
by your sport and generosity.

What you really think is that by being lavish
you can buy friendship,
and you spread around your sorrow
like meal to the hens,
to the hard selected ruffians
hand out your soft self.

And, though you have it right,
for money does indeed
banish all pride, all determination,
if you could only see
the further temptation
which lies down on the road sadly
waiting to help...

From your high tower
use another telescope,
and you will see that the soldiers
are mere fantasy,
or worse still victims,
the delight of boors,

and that the same raw material
makes their heart move as yours…

THE SHEPHERD

The sheep while searching found
a hole in the fence,
sniffed around it for a while
and then went through.

She went on a long straying journey,
and when she turned
to retrace her steps
the way back was beyond her.

She stood there in a daze,
and a new scent came to her big soft nostrils,
she threw a jerking eye around,
and knew that something strange and savage
had been found.

She fled, not knowing where,
and the wolf followed
with bloody throat heaving,
the chase was long and hard
and would have had the inevitable result
as the sheep finally collapsed
had not the shepherd
arrived in his searching
at the critical moment.

The fierce one, too,
stopped in mid-stride –
then coursed around
at a slight distance
a panting circle,

and gurgled in its head,
and jumped for no reason into the air
before withdrawing backwards
into the forest.

The shepherd took the sheep on his shoulders
and took it back to safety,
back to the warm and cosy fold,
rejoicing of course
for the one which was lost,
now safe with the flock.

But he forgot to mend
the hole in the fence…

THE ROUNDABOUT WAY

Over ridges and plains and gentle mounds
the great roads, three in number, run –
the lighted road on which walks the white bull,
the rain-swept road where stamps the dun,
and on the hidden road starting to race
shuffles the black bull devoid of grace.

At the highest hillock where all the roads meet
silence reigns
regal,
strong,
serene.

That is where all alone I stand
while the blood is draining
in metre straining
to the dead centre
of my heart.

TO A RURAL HAMLET

High stones bright
in the dark of night
on black earth standing,
time's light fading
as fog settles evenly on rock.

Silence without sorrow
for those who remain,
and the mystery of those who were taken
over the impregnable fence
– the eyes of the ignorant
don't know why,
but there was a reason,
some reason somehow.

I noticed that reason
in the used rosary beads
on an old woman's fingers
on a wintry night
as the dank weather moaned
outside a lone chapel,
and the snipe of death
called long from the wild.

The reason I noted again
written on the level land
one evening at the crossroads opposite the tavern
– weak voices, strong voices, mingled,
and the strongest were in command.

The reason lit up

through a stained-glasss window
before the altar
and the dull slanting ray
over the heads of people
with the colour of ages.

But the reason was troubled
when new ways were seen,
the handy shortcuts,
and one who broke away,
and was followed by another and another,
so that almost all the people
soon were gone.

And the reason never came to life again
except near the crossroads long after midnight
when an unseen cock crowed,
and a male hand
found a female bland,
and youth came again to life
on its very own course
to die.

And, because of that,
all sense was lost
on a cold windy morning
under a lemon sky,
on the little twisted road,
when high heels were clicking
in the direction of cities.

A whirl thereafter,
as never before,
difference in epochs other lands,
difference in accents other hands,
difference in distance other pleasures,
difference in people other treasures.

But always remaining,
to return to,
a broken cross
was lifted high on the ditch of three boundaries,
grave of the still-born,
a place dead from hoping,

where the restless eye
coursed all around seeking
but always returned
to stare stonily on the road.

Still the picture of a woman
who used to come in black shawl at nightfall
to standing stones on a darkened bank
praying in an opening,
crying her breast
for a world which had lost its colour
when she suffered her own loss
years ago, and was left barren.

If I said her poem
my words would pulsate so,
for they could not be denied,
they would stand so defiant,
and my eyes would not be on confusion,
on the surly cheek and greedy ear,
on the multiple wheel-turning
which grinds mills of God,
on the cowled figures
passing through a landscape
through a grassy trodden laneway
between black trees
on
to a sunlight which beckons,
but no signposts on the road.

And my mind would not be
on a dour high ceiling
with fearsome old paint
from which screams of terror rise,
and figures being shovelled
in their sweatiness and bloodiness
to a hole bolted in mystery,
to a flaming oven where words burn.

But I would sing a lamentation
in words of cut stone,
on what dies in people,
on the souring and ruin,
on dreadful twists of the way

and images gone totally astray.

A verse would be on my lips
which lived on in the elements,
like ice for dexterity,
like light in the sea,
that all things are truth
– the red earth, the clear water,
the wild air
and a body which once was alive
and moved without rancour to death –
the face of the dying
filling the sky.

THE COMING

High among the crags
between the jutting rocks
in a place so empty
in twilight,
all was a vacuum
like a ghost who never lived.

And then a crash of silence
and you were there,
and underneath you a horse,
its sides in motion,
its mouth all frothy,
its head dancing on the rein
held by your right hand.

After our long wait
you were approaching,
and the town was already
with flames
harsh
crackling and roaring.

SMUGNESS

These people, you know who I mean,
never listen to the glory
of the speaking voice
of man,
and therefore they let him die,
and when he is gone
they remember that his high rhetoric
lacked any meaning,
or that it is dated,
or just not available.

And so they ignore someone
who is gone in the head,
because that makes them feel better –
the madness, you see –
and, perhaps even without realising it,
they hate people
because they are dead.

But nobody ever was dead,
but a poet and brother
could make him rise again...

ETERNAL CIRCLE

Run around, you ball impenetrable…
run around, you sleek dark metal…
run through glints of sunlight peeping…
run around the icy pole.

TOO LATE

Talking is a strange thing
– just when a hush shows people are listening
the barman shouts 'Time up!'
and makes all sorts of noise.

Noise is a stranger thing,
the teaching voice
– just when people are beginning to learn
the exams are over
and all rush off to life.

Life is a strange thing indeed
– just when you are getting the hang of it,
a gibbet marks the skyline.

THE MEANINGS

Would you think it odd if I were now to tell you
that I have still kept by the piece of slate,
in a quiet place,
where you wrote down a verse a night we were together
not dreaming that it would be kept this way
for that was not the reason why you wrote it there.

And now that you have found a different focus
than long ago when you were without care,
and all the signs you follow read like jumbles
to me who has not quite forgotten where
you wrote a poem which one alone can bear.

THE SOLITARY

A being is walking
through the night,
footsteps are biting
into the dark, the hungry.

Outside of the temple
where the crowds gather
the shoes are sounding
on the black frost.

The people inside
are leaving now
so politely –
one here, one there,
the shaking of hands so neatly,
and the warm chatter.

When they hear the footsteps
coming in strange but human shape,
they look towards it
to scrutinise the features.

And the strong voice speaks
from their midst shrewd and experienced,
and he hears it:
'Who is that snooping around?'

'What is his excuse
– we know there is always one –
for being abroad at this hour of night,
the shadow passed through the gate just now,

the hand is grasping something,
the harm is lurking?'

Loudly again speaks that voice,
more sharply this time,
growing in authority,
and the shade replies
oddly and low:

'I am a lost spirit searching,
in straight lines and circles,
always on my course,
seeking a candle…

But don't you be worried,
now,
I am just passing by,
I may not even return —
the deep night will find me
far away from your town…'

SLIPPING AWAY

The sky is so motionless,
like a donkey on strike,
or a hound watching a hare,
or a miser thinking money.

But a lone man is waving
furiously like a lunatic,
while under his feet
the very sod stirs…

The ground is in motion,
the great sea stands still,
but to that man in silhouette
the opposite holds true…

He threatens
all alone,
with hand, mouth, his very blood,
but silence lies a coarse clean blanket
on the sky, on the water…

My eyes become shaded
and this sight is swallowed
in the swampland of memory –
the little man full of fervour
while time gurgles on…

BARD OF A DISTANT PAST

The sun returns today from her shadows damp and pale,
on silent feet still creeping from the land where death prevails,
in the chill of this quiet morning she doesn't look so fair,
but the soft strength is edging and dripping through each vein.

That dreariness and vigour, that decay and that growth,
are a feeling and a freshness that were there long ago,
always reeling, always whirling, and coming in new clothes
through all the things and beings which pulsate forever more.

On this same mountain vista on a quiet ancient day
the terrain was like this one except that growth was not spared,
the great elk's antler was marking time on a young sun's face
and the dull thud of mammoth feet shook the ground over there.

An old chain wends its way through a mind-washing stream,
morning light on every turn rekindles primal dreams…

VIEW FROM A ROOM

Away on the mountains
the loud rain is falling,
a green sheet stretching
from these rooftops through unbroken air.

Away on the mountains
a pretty girl, I think, is sheltering,
or an old woman in the gathering storm,
but her mouth is so worn
and my picture is torn.

The mountains are far away,
but I long to walk out there,
on the long rocky roadways
from this window far away.

For those hills extermination,
someone calls it liberation…

141

HOPE BY THE HEDGEROWS

I saw you riding down along by hedges
going out to the noise-ridden plain,
to a broad countryside full of fashion and of favour,
disappearing along the edge of my mind I saw you go.

And how I heard the pounding of hooves upon hard earth,
beating out a tune in music harsh and raw!
I saw your head, or at least its back, as you departed –
a face more beautiful than that I never saw.

BORING

I tend to be digging holes in the ground
all over my garden
– each hole is then empty,
so I measure it,
and every one of them I dig out
increases in size threefold
exactly.

I imagine then that if I went deeper
that I would begin to understand each clod,
each ridge, each line, each rock and decayed rag
which jumps up at me from the earth,
and this hidden knowledge which illumines all;
but I just get more dejected, more tormented,
and so I tear my hair
and scratch the white flesh on my forehead,
and root down even deeper still.

The thought
to find a hole without rot or slime,
without border or end.
always clean, neatly formed...

But instead my lone discovery
in holes great or small
is that every body is quietly
tearing and being torn,
and each cut pours blood up through the soil towards me,
through some opening,
whether narrow or broad.

Until the bottom of the hole be someday reached

at the root of every effort,
and there no longer is a vacuum waiting,
but instead a crusted corner
where lives
all alone and alienated
the paradox fumbling and sniffing,
a striped animal locked there
in its ferocity,
staring up with eyes so cold
yet so wild,
sending signs and echoes upwards
through every rung
of life.

NO ANALYSIS!

A broad green vacant field
in a cloud without colour,
the space is empty, cold, and clean,
and my sight becomes dizzy;
I am running for my life –
strange life that it is –
racing like a crumbling stone
up the slope where athletes groan.

The wicked black bull,
angry and bitter of tongue,
whose meaning I don't conceive,
but know, and this suffices,
that he gives
the sign of fear.

All at once is the impact,
the fence, the bull, and myself,
as if all was from the beginning bound to happen
– this again and again into which we return
and look for a reason before we scream –
and if I don't wake up from my dream now
what will be there for you to read?

Regardless of all the men in glasses,
and their laboratories and marking-up sheets,
and papers to be delivered on the personality
and twists of sex and the environment,
and the sudden and lasting paralysis of mind,
I know that it is no murky clammy spectre once experienced

which torments me so tonight.

But horror from an ancient world
which comes before its time –
the savage old black bull
bellowing to the skies.

ON THE COAST OF CLARE

Out there in the west there lies an island
still and strong in red flecks piercing
in the evening
mid a calming sea...

the boat drifts to a tiny harbour,
at the very end of archways,
where wavelets soothe the rocks by touching,
softly stroking,
easing
frothing mouths of sea-lions
foaming...

and there too, slowly,
comb-toothed
jet-propelling
wearied
whales
whose tender voices race
through humped-backed seas and arching fathoms,
go to their retreat,
rest there in their time-conditioned
solemn sleep...

on the island stands a castle
the causeway to it long and narrow,
the gate lies open and unguarded,
but the door is locked
to me...

a chilly mountain lake here generating

electric streams and shocks to teeth,
somewhere deep down in its bottom
lies the key...

A TRIP BEGINS AND ENDS

By that wide harbour once I saw
the prophet walk
up from the seafront –
his clothes, his hair, all his person
were of a bright colour as if shining,
and his little band of followers
followed on as was their wont
kindly smiling, softly whispering,
walking in from the sea,
he raised his hand...

They left their boats outside
nine waves from the shore
and walked through the rest of the water
on sandalled feet,
coming upwards towards the jetty
where the crowd waited –
all the mouths fell open
in expectation of yet another wonder
or of some new doctrine
from the depths of the sea.

He came to them,
walking right through them,
all the eyes followed him...

A little later the words were heard
which caused all ears to awaken
stretching in hope for something new,
hungrily greedily
longing for the story from the east;

he stopped by a standing stone
which had stood there surviving
from the mists of history,
he sat there and spoke...

But the soft words did not rub
against the hairy hands
of the mind,
and greater was the attention given
to the colour of his eyes,
deep blue of the sea in their centre,
white crystal of the waves in the edges
of the eyes which brightened out
to cover all...

At the ancient standing-stone
the dark shape of a pondering spirit
was seen to sink to earth,
that spirit which had possessed the place,
and the crash of battle lessened
until it died away altogether,
no longer a vile nest there
of killing and slaughter and cutting
which had held the whip-hand for so long,
ever since the two maddened groups
faced each other ferociously,
gnashing their teeth and seeping saliva
with hate and deadened eyes
as the taste of blood grew hot and red...

The prophet came from the ocean,
his voice drove away the demons,
he sent away on a foreign range
the shades of history groaning,
the agents of battle banished,
their weapons stopped in the air
and – only to be a memory – remained there.

And when he approached the city,
wending the well-trodden way
which, young again now, shouted a welcome
to the heroes of all-white clothes,
the multitude clustered
on each pathway,

having come from playing-fields and business-desks,
walking now step by step with prophets
who had come from far away,
walking over bridges and through traffic-lights,
past beautiful multi-storied houses whitewashed...

The budding blossoms burst forth on every side
of their own accord,
celebrating their bright new birth,
white and purple and scarlet they grew,
also blue,
till they spread in an explosion of flowers,
and the stones moistened,
shining on their tops the honey trickled forth,
and the old tree which had lingered in death for ages
in the corner under a load of shadows
began to green and grow again...

Under their feet when touched by them
some of the stones moved for a moment
and turned to gold...

He went to the temple without delay
and, in quite a matter-of-fact way,
walked right in
and knocked down the idols,
dashing their skulls of darkened stone,
and then he took a piece of cloth
and cleaned up every spot of blood
with red rims and black clodded centres
which once had stained the horrid walls,
shed by victims,
and every ugly sound was silenced
from every shameful psalm,
and the druids of malice were quietened,
and the clutching harlots frightened,
and the spirit-drink which cuts all throats
was just flung away there
out through the doors...

Every mouth hung loose with longing
as he gave them the teaching –
how this was but a foresign
of what yet might come to pass,

and how still they might face bad times,
how to be eternally watchful;
they knew, they knew, this catchcry,
but then quite out of the blue
he moved on to a different tune,
how not to place trust in those with money
who would come and smile in private,
puffed with pride and fine clothes,
causing dissensions and uproars;
they must keep away from them, give them a wide berth,
and, if necessary, retreat into the desert,
and no harm would come
to those who stayed apart
looking to themselves,
and – above all else – to protect the books,
hide them as a last resort
in scattered caves on the tops of mountains
or deep in caverns underneath the earth,
and down through the fog of years
these books would once again appear…

If they would follow this course
all would be renewed some day,
and the city would once again be brightened,
the buildings high and proud and shining,
and paving of gold underneath each foot,
and horses shod in gold,
and lush gardens a delirium of colour stretching far and near,
all in the care of the bare old temple,
and all the scholars together
reading the books in earnest
for the first time ever
without malice or envy,
and every etched letter would inspire an image
to fill and fire the mind
in a people who had long shook hands with tricksters,
who had long been pillaged.

Everybody listened to those words,
but some were no longer so impressed,
to them it might be right but they saw no point
in all the doom and gloom about what might happen,
the world was not so bad
and time would heal all evils;

but a smaller number grouped together
and followed him away to the desert,
into a place which no-one knew,
and he was drowned there by accident
in a small whirlpool unchartered,
which they suddenly came upon
as if it had come upon them,
as they crossed a river of marvels
where it flowed by wisdom's margins.

And when they returned to their homes
the weeds had grown,
the white dried earth unsown,
and all the working-loads
stood blandly there alone
like ghost-infested houses,
like deserted spouses,
no food had been prepared,
no money earned, no wage,
the debts were all unpaid,
the schools had been neglected,
children saucy full of impudence
and cool rehearsed rejection,
and the old old questions came to haunt them
from graveyards overgrown with staunch old weeds,
and arrangements had still to be made
each day which came
as the sun renewed its rays…

And they stopped and looked
at each other…

THOSE WHO ENDURE

A voice has many ways to earn a living
as it travels through the body
from crashing waves,
once projected outwards onto the world,
a pulse in the air pushes and surrenders,
or even on electrolysed tape
sparking on the pivot,
or going wild into regions outside the sky
where no ear is at hand to hear it, or no eye.

Sometimes it lives as cuts on parchment,
a half-echo in writing thrown from one surface,
from a rendable rock.

Yet when a trace of one voice survived
it only was speech with no polish or style,
such was of course
encasing it in philosophy
− of later date −
but for itself it merely strove to be
and lived like a shell in a slanting sea
or a vein touching coldness, sensing an ending…

Its accent was not really broadcastable,
no proclamation,
nor what we all crave of praising and blaming,
no deep meanings from the logical fort,
in the formulae of scholars
or in interest's worth…

But only a few little words,

in an alley through which a merciless wind blows,
a few little words
shivering all alone…

Do not put two coats on you
– thus he spoke.

TWO IMAGES AND A CHOICE

Stare at the fresco,
at the lines straightening out in every direction
from the one who walks right out of the tomb,
as the enemies fall away on every side
backwards,
and noting the left hand raised in announcement
– one eye is the very centre of the light,
but the other above the cheek
is engulfed by a lengthening shade.

Do not let one hand know
what the other hand is doing...

You too may once meet another
– the man with the tail in the desert,
who speaks to you in soft and very personal tones
intended as some kind of challenge,
though exactly which kind you hardly will know,
and he tempts you amid the burning sand,
saying that all before you should be a prize,
all this and more
which will yet give you your fill in the end,
that thousands of years can be laid aside with no bother
and that the forty days should be spent in absolute rapture,
then he will give you a dig in the shoulder
and a knowing wink,
enticing you to tricks quite new to you,
and let his eyes drift towards shivering wonders
which are awaiting
with very few conditions attached.

You look down at one of your hands, and then at the other,
close one blinking eye mid that fine preview…

Then stare again with the two eyes drawn together
at the huge white mushroom rising proudly to the sky
shattering all at its roots,
and all the helpless pigs a-screeching
as their skin is torn away in a blinding flash,
ripped to the very bone,
with the testing fire preparing one destruction,
and all the neat plans which have been drawn up
for what might follow,
and what is the destined lot of each of his own…

You begin to hear the new rain
the dirty piercing rain
spreading from the horizon over all,
and then you look again
on the absolutely still but yellow sand…

The son of curses
who knows each draft and plan and method,
and the son of man
who knows not where to lay his head…

RETURNING TO A PLACE

That was twenty years ago —
the knife-sharp rain penetrated us,
the river stretched before us
as it climbed into the hills,
a ragged white line,
little fish lingered under the water
— that was twenty years ago.

And every footstep you took
on another white line,
the low cement wall beside your pathway
stretching back into the mist of evening,
every footstep,
and look…
we are here again.

158

CHIMERA IN THE SKY

Thinking of the poet as mason
who comes unknown from the silent places
to an ancient city with white walls,
where a tall ship with billowing sails
lies docked for years at the quayside.

And then I see the gaping hole
where no nail had been driven,
high up in its prow,
just a little below the deck,
where no human hand could reach it
either from above or below
without paying the veering price
of slipping and giving way,
and down to where the ship begins,
careering towards the bawling sea,
towards the terrible crushing
and the quiet thud of death.

But I catch a nail, fling it into the air,
and swing the great mallet
around my shoulders,
the only one left,
rusty with years,
release it on high –
up it goes
like a heavy lark which does not twitter,
it strikes the nail
of its own accord as if seeking it
with its nose,
away above,

and wedges it into the notch.

The ship slides from the quay,
poet also me…

THE HORSE-LOVER

Eochaidh the sun-god paces across the heavens in the form of a horse each day. Eochaidh was in love with the beautiful Étaín, she of the enchanting voice who caused the land to flower; but she was transformed into a butterfly and blown away by the wind. Her radiance dazzled him, and he searched long and sadly for her, clearing plains and levelling forests, but all in vain:

Rocks and trees in the still cold morning,
kissed by departing mist they wake,
life stirs in the verdant valley –
you, white steed, begin your race;

as you move your eye reflects it sideways –
light through forest's deepest route,
where she dances without ceasing ever,
making all the flowers bloom
into myriads of colours shading,
petals red through gold and blue,
with scented violet all her shape is gleaming,
startled wings attracting
every hue

– you watched and saw,
she floated on the air,
her voice was soft and clear,
one moment, then was gone –

so you always travel westwards
towards the sea which sways beside the land,
brightened once by life-drenched
sunbursts,
shadows dying slowly on the sand;

the great horse leaves the valley,
down by the sloping shore
into the ocean,
walks over onto his far island,
enters his lonely chamber
shining;

bright sun,
great lover left in silence,
in your own primeval home,
long to hear the rising voices,
hope among them
for one note...

PLAN OF HUNDRED DAYS

Fionn Mac Cumhaill, hero and seer, sent the runner Caoilte to collect for him all the living things of Ireland and bring them to Tara where Fionn himself was imprisoned. Caoilte did this, and further showed his skill by keeping a dozen hares all night in a house with a dozen open doors:

Away with you through the greying valleys,
have your bags well packed with food,
walk the cantreds on hill and level,
and come not back without your loot.

You have your instructions – do not deny them –
collect together all that you find,
the sun dancing on ridges betokens good fortune
and the grass lying still under a waxing moon –
cease from your travels only with a failing footstep,
and quicken your pace again when revived,
and as you receive them, so bring all to me
and I will rule on the evidence gleaned,
on things that now live or are escaping towards being.

Every creature which moves on four measured feet,
darting towards you or fleeing in terror,
every leaf even, count out its tendons,
every tree and each budding reckon for me,
all those in need or in heat or in pulsing
I will gather here where I am
in my knotty old clutch,
every picture I love
of each white cooing dove,
every twitch in the breast.

And you, o runner who has vanquished all,
who leaves your competitors panting and prostrate,
you who out-tortoise,
no Achilles you without end comprehended,
but a silent force with head bent to shoulders,
a flash in the morning and then you are gone,
Caoilte the slender, Caoilte the speedy,
who moves just as fast
as the mind of a woman
or as man's ambition,
set your foot to the road and gather your swiftness,
you who will bring to me the errant ones,
the squirrel in your sock slipped over its head,
the grasshopper prating and the fugitive wren,
the bird in flight,
the stallion on his mares,
the bull midst his herd,
the great stag bellowing and rising to the new sun,
the hare who gives ear to you,
the reverend badger and recluse hedgehog.

Then swim without fear to the five-pointed otter
who rules without wounding as lord of the torrent,
as king of the cold realm
who enkindles no greed,
yet for fear of a rival
he never will sleep.

Nor dare you forget the druid,
lest the druid forsake you,
as he forsook them long ago and was killed on the way,
the red-haired one who attracts all attention
and but for that would always succeed
where others always fail,
remember him
whether human or not,
whether biped or fox
– see him, notice him,
breathe him, quote from him…

When seen
going through the wide fields
as Lovernios the fox
he will draw, great artist that he is,

his own picture
— a shape slinking russet
against the green leaves
moving…

Then, without parchment…

His sniffing and tricking
give dimension to greed,
his legs and brush letters
a prophet can read,
from his sudden quick running
ahead of the deed
we'll decipher from slyness
all that we need.

Do not neglect even the deep one,
the ordinary man, most elusive of all —
speak little to him for fear he might hide,
coax him, cajole him rather than force him,
you must never punish him even for pride;
but bring at all costs whether free or in shackles,
his great sins have not yet ruled him out of the pack,
though many's the time he has earned stark rejection,
and danger to him lies in denying his luck —
yet will I drink from the pool of his wishes,
his pain and his sorrow though short-lived his kind,
what spurs him so fast on from giving to taking…
grab from him every mite of his mind…

Lead him in, and leave him before me
stark, bare, and naked
on this old plate on this old table,
so that I be satisfied without being pleased
with the broken slate of his dreams.

All the darkest thoughts that live for a while,
and then every blushing on face will be felt,
the thoughts which turn quickly from burning to action,
the shiver in isolation,
the lonely cry at dawn
which swells to multitudes gathered together
when one is lost to all,
and thrills for a time, .

then returns to its norm
– bring me this message,
and then I myself will go.

I will go in the form of all the mammals
learning the laws not yet imagined
by the one who lives with poverty's sting
from the king to the ragged and from ragged to king,
and my eyes will penetrate
even to blindness
the hills and the valleys and streamlets,
the movements the stirrings the weakness,
riding each picture as a wild horse rearing,
chafing at the bit,
and I'll drink the milk of a thousand cows
racing like electric pulse to my mouth,
in the timeless hope that the world and its fun
may be laid at the feet of the loneliest one,
all the shapes growing cold
in this silly new theatre
here with all the props
but the lights put out,
where nothing is heard
but the nightwatchman's shout…

In the deserted dwelling I now abide
singing my poem with quiet desire…

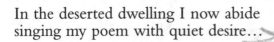

INDEX OF FIRST LINES

Typesetting by **Elefthæria Machæras**
ARTELIER, 6 Kratilou St., 104 42, Athens, Greece
Tel./Fax : ++30 1 515 46 43

printed and bound by **EUROPRINT: Ath. E. Petroulakis S.A.**
3km Koropi - Vari Av. 19400, Athens, Greece
Tel : ++30 1 602 22 42-5/602 00 11   Fax : ++30 1 662 39 57
e-mail : info@europrint.gr

for **Philomel Productions Ltd**, Dublin, Republic of Ireland
England contact address : 1 Queen's Gate Place Mews
                    London SW7 5BG, England, UK
                    Tel : ++44 (0) 20 7581 2303
                    Fax : ++44 (0) 20 7589 2264
Ireland contact address : e-mail: oriagain@gofree.indigo.ie

Book cover design and artwork : Christos Georgiou
Book design : Sophia Kakkavas

ISBN 1 898685 30 4
2001